ANIMAL

COLORING BOOKS

FOR TEENS

COLOR TEST PAGE

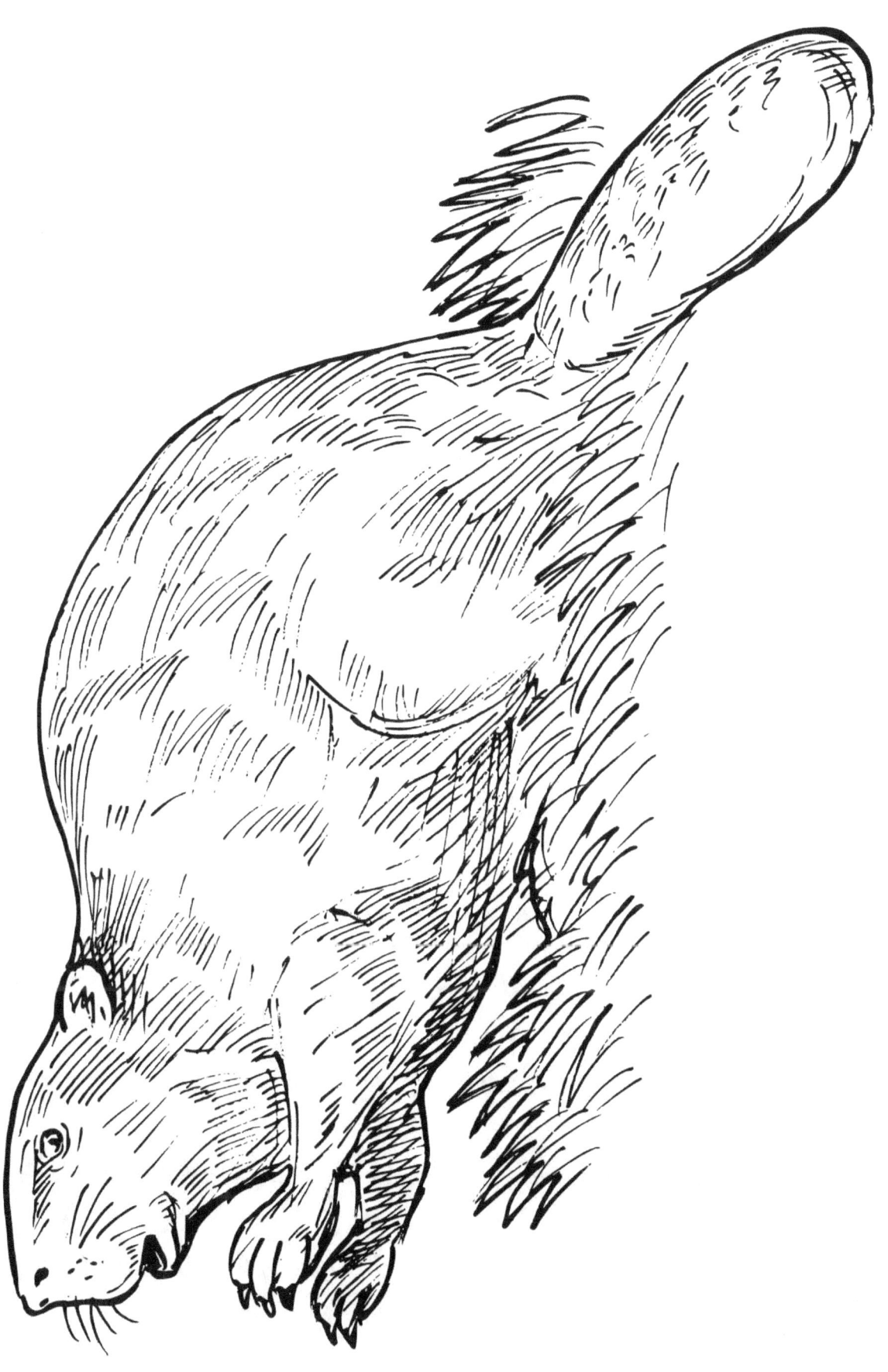

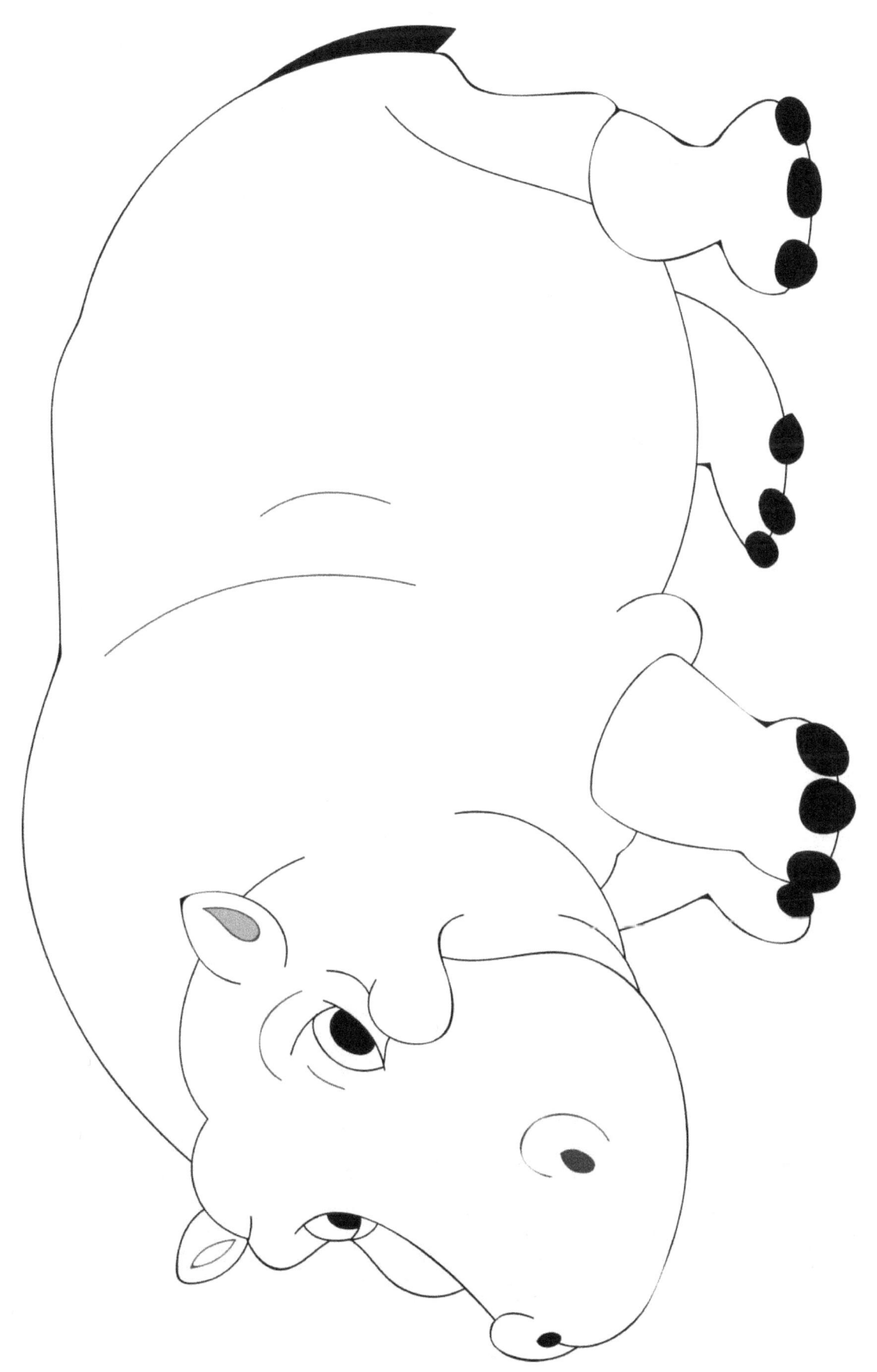

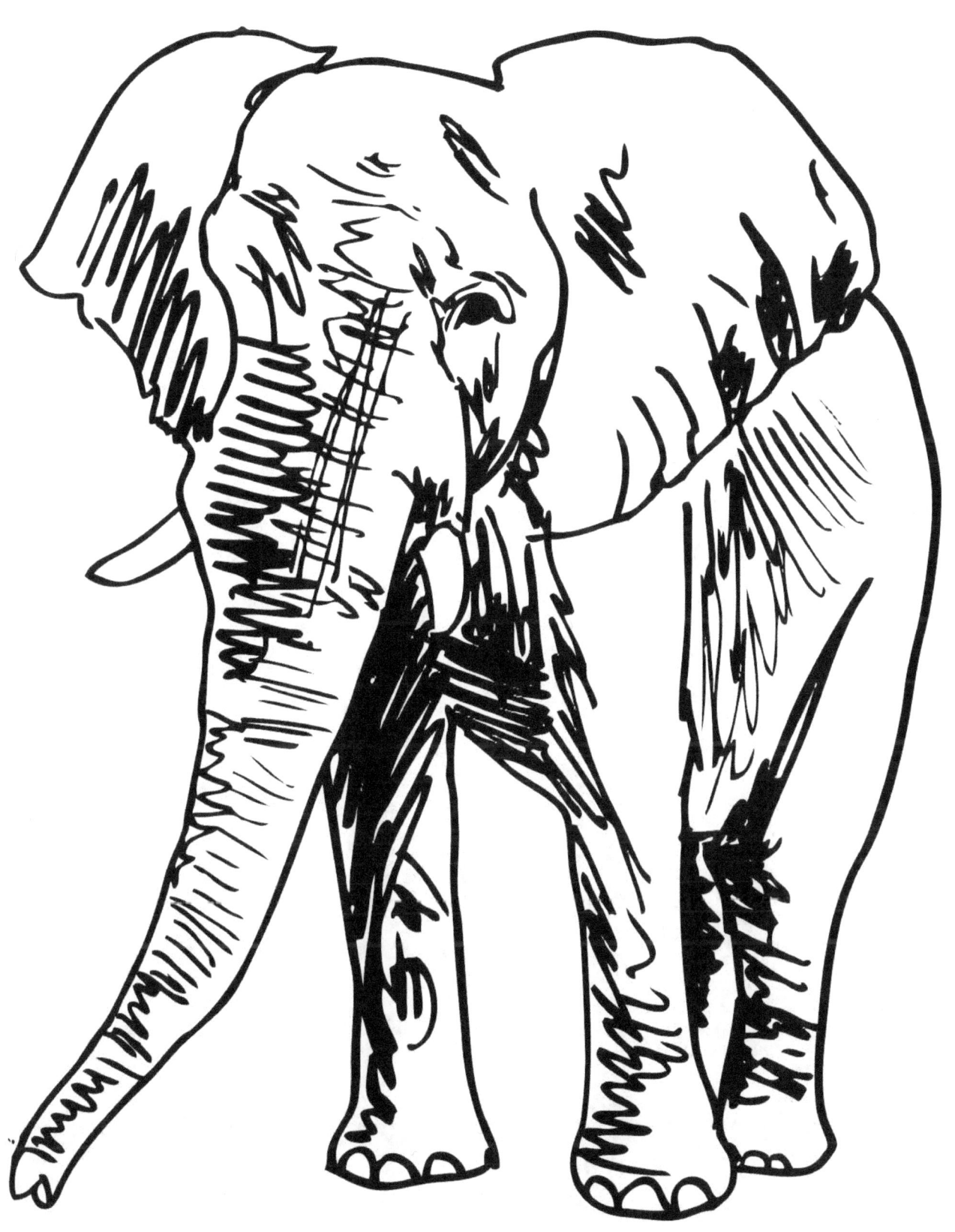

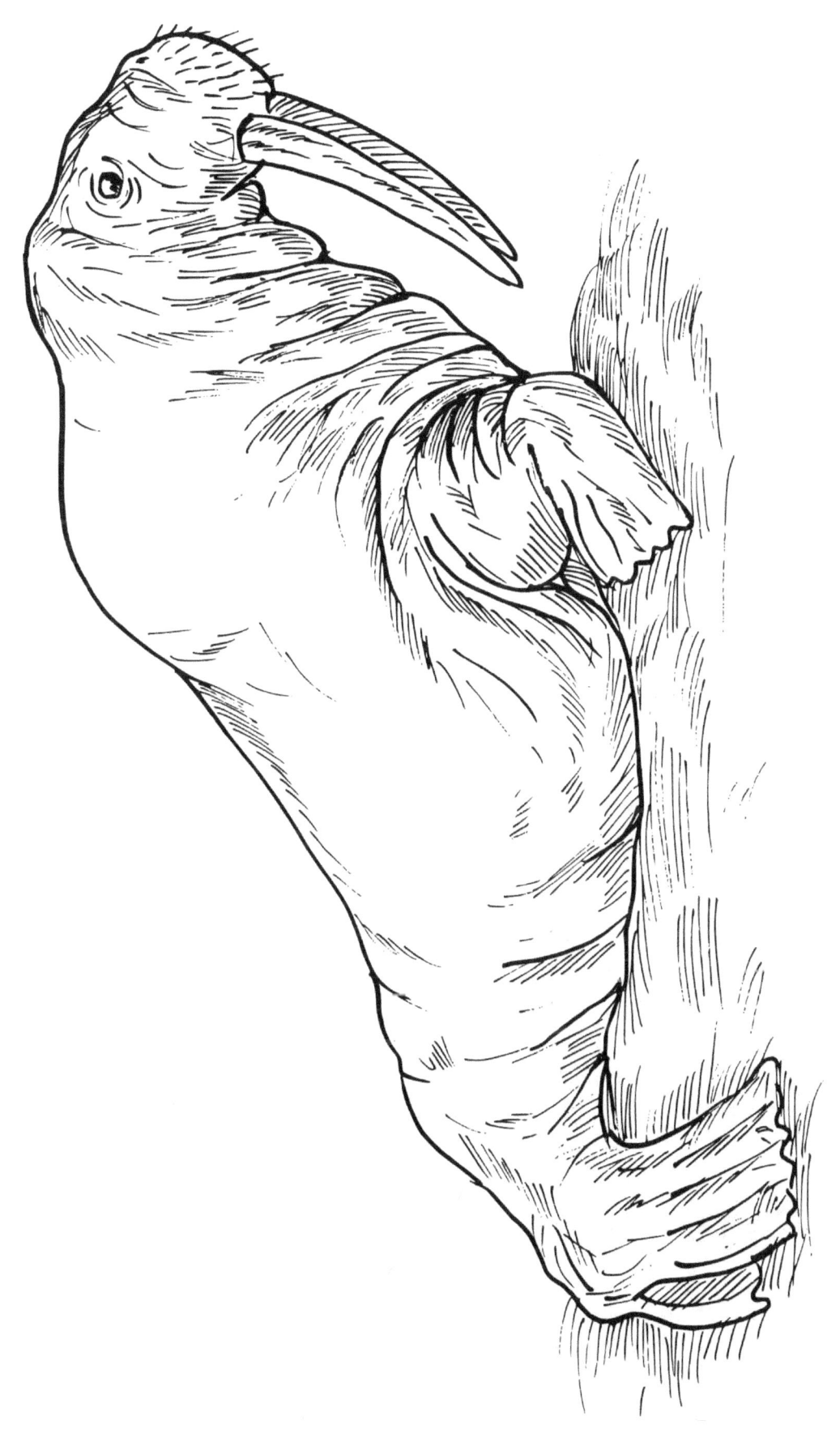

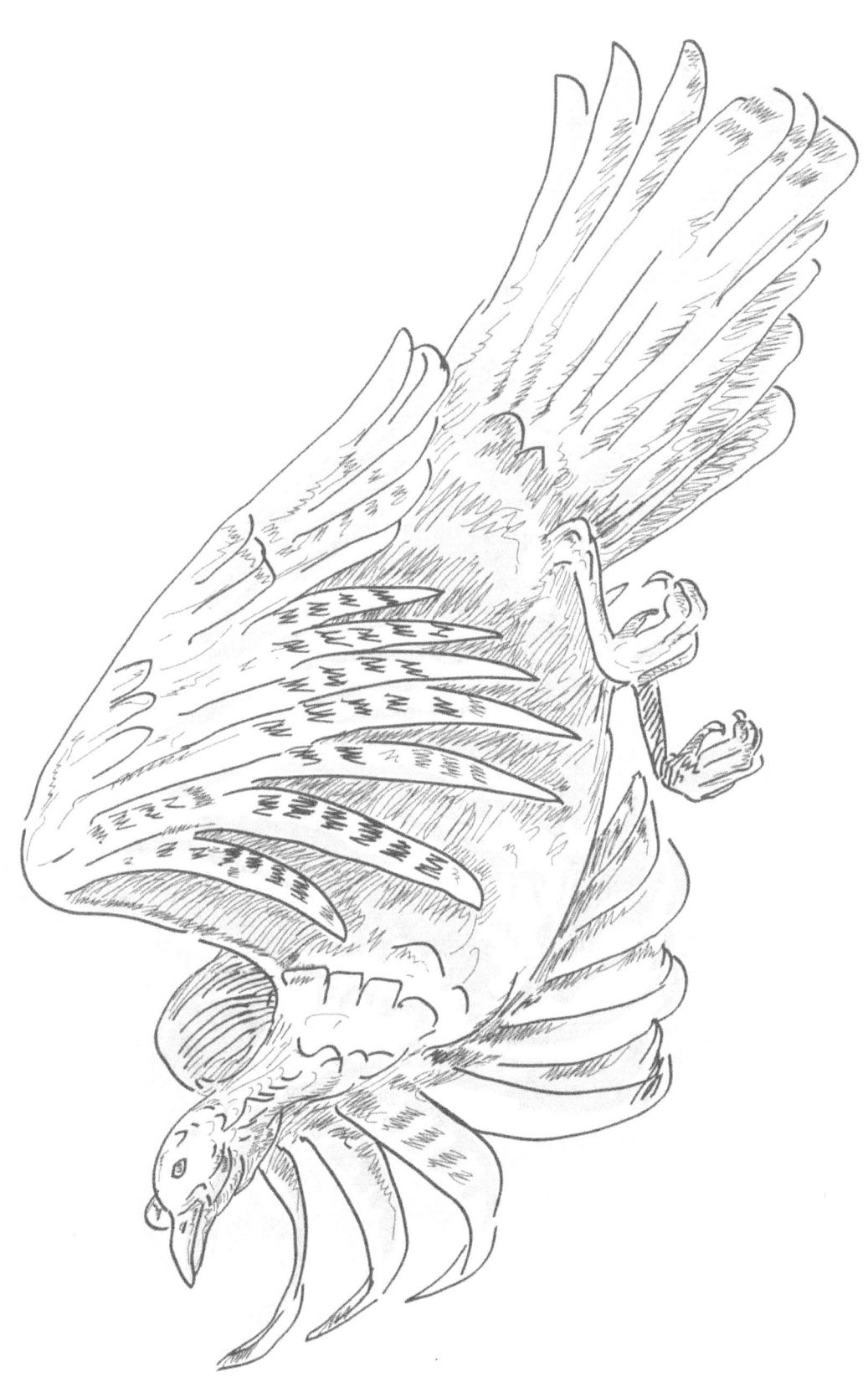

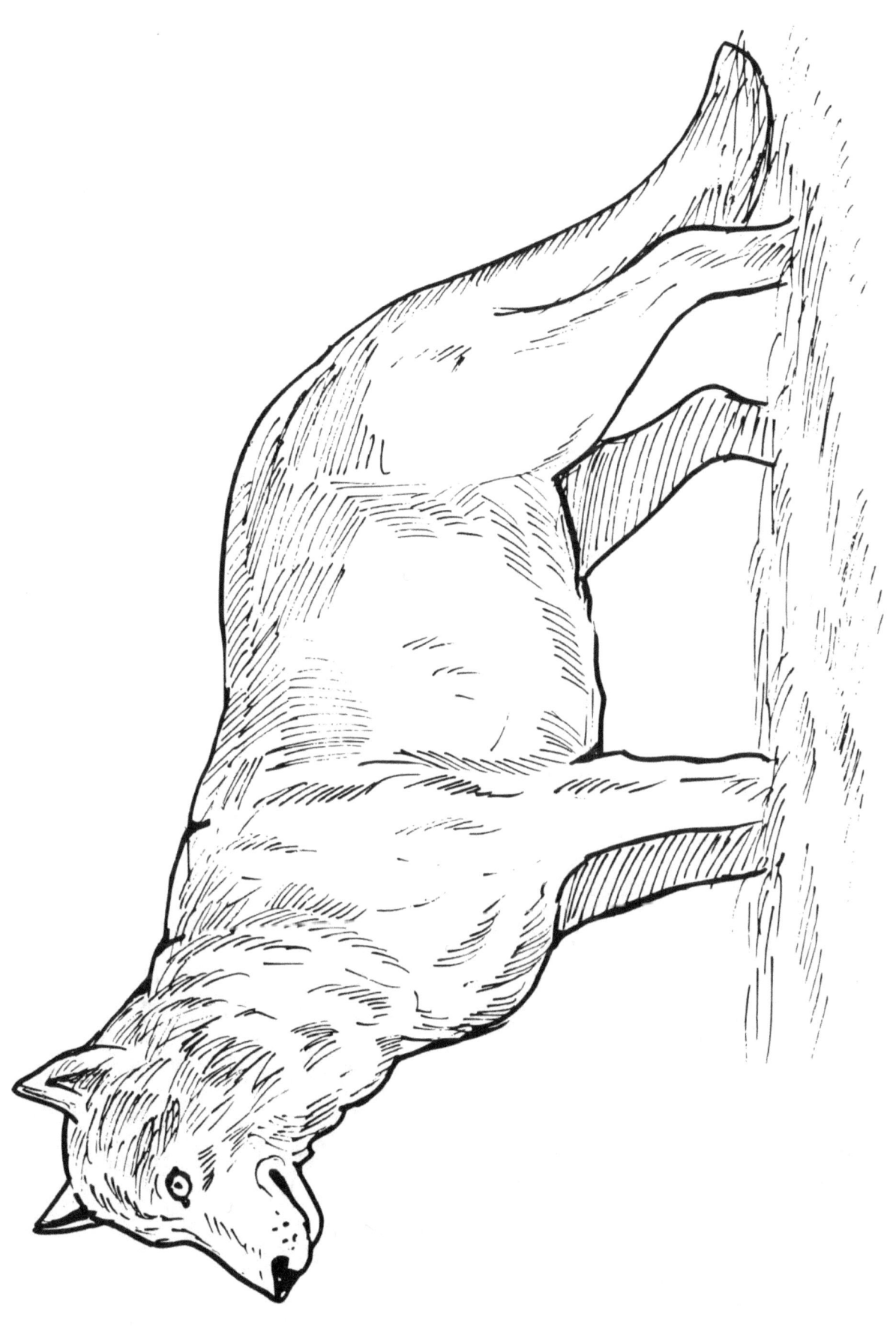

ZEBRA

www.ingramcontent.com/pod-product-compliance
Lightning Source LLC
Chambersburg PA
CBHW081118280526

45787CB00007B/2883

* 9 7 8 1 5 3 5 1 5 8 0 9 1 *